I0449700

SKETCH BOOK

www.ingramcontent.com/pod-product-compliance
Lightning Source LLC
Chambersburg PA
CBHW081552280526
45788CB00011B/3457
9781096849742